PAKORAS, PANEER, PAPPADUMS:

A GUIDE TO INDIAN RESTAURANT MENUS

Colleen Taylor Sen

Acknowledgements:

This handbook wouldn't have seen the light of day without the support and suggestions of my husband, Ashish Sen. I am extremely grateful to Helen Saberi and Bonnie Feingold for their very helpful comments and suggestions, as well as to Sharon Durr, S. Biswas, Mr. Sayeed (Bhabi's Kitchen), and Sanjeev Pandey (Indian Harvest Restaurant). Of course, any mistakes are entirely my own.

Design: Christy Michals

Photo Credits: Jiayang Yuan/iStockphoto, p1 (tandoori chicken); Linda and Colin McKie/iStockphoto, pp1 (chicken tikka masala), 7, 14 (vindaloo), 16 (meen molee), 22, 24, 28; Elizabeth Shoemaker/iStockphoto, p2; Joe Gough/Bigstockphoto, pp3, p31; Joe Gough/iStockphoto, p13 (gobi), p15 (vindaloo), p17 (pilao); Romanus/iStockphoto, p5; Chris Schmidt/iStockphoto, p8; ©2005, nickgraywfu, p9; Courtesy Rasika, p11; Ashwin K. Abhirama/Bigstockphoto, p12 (thali); ©2009 Miansarin55, p12 (samosas); Elena Moiseeva/Bigstockphoto, p13 (bhelpuri); courtesy Curry House, p15 (various kababs); Nilesh Bhange/Bigstockphoto, p17 (dosas); Vazhapully Bhaskaran Baiju/Bigstockphoto, p18 (mango pickle); Elzbieta Sekowska/iStockphoto, pp18 (puris), p23; Umbar Shakir/iStockphoto, p19 (burfi); courtesy Curry House, p19 (gulab jaman); Eva Gruendemann/iStockphoto, p20; courtesy Indian Harvests (p29)

Table of Contents

(continued)

The purpose of this guide is to help the diner interpret the menu of Indian restaurants in North America and choose dishes that will not only expand their understanding but also enhance their enjoyment of a great world cuisine.

The food of the Indian subcontinent (which includes India, Bangladesh, Pakistan and Nepal) remains an enigma for many North Americans. Diners who can comfortably navigate a Chinese or Thai menu may find themselves at sea when faced with the choices in an Indian restaurant. Some waiters are reluctant to explain dishes to customers or make suggestions about what they should order. Some diners are afraid that Indian dishes will be mouth-searingly hot (although this is rarely the case). And, unlike Chinese restaurants, Indian restaurants do not offer 'set meals' for groups, although some do offer individual 'thalis'—a selection of main dishes and condiments in little bowls on a round tray—and buffets, especially at lunch.

Tandoori chicken

As a result, many diners limit themselves to ordering a few dishes. Restaurant owners told me that the majority of their customers order just three entrees: tandoori chicken, butter chicken or chicken tikka masala (pieces of grilled chicken in a creamy tomato sauce), and sag or palak paneer (spinach with farmer's cheese).

Chicken tikka masala

This bewilderment is understandable. For one thing, there's really no such thing as Indian cuisine. India is an enormous country with 24 official languages, eight religions, and a multitude of ethnic and social divisions. Regional culinary differences are far greater than in Europe.

Palak paneer

Moreover, India does not have a long tradition of dining outside the home. Religious and social beliefs restricted what one could eat, who could prepare it, and with whom one could eat. Eating out was tolerated largely as a necessity rather than valued as a luxury or new experience.

Unlike a Western meal, a traditional Indian meal does not have separate courses—appetizers, entrees, side dishes, salads, and desserts. This meant that restaurant proprietors had to create menus to conform to Western eating patterns. The resulting menu is a hodgepodge of dishes from different regions and traditions ranging from street food and home cooking to the lofty regions of haute cuisine.

I hope this little guidebook will give readers a better understanding of this delicious cuisine and the wonderful establishments that serve it.

What is an Indian Meal?

Defining a typical Indian meal is very difficult in view of the enormous physical, climatic, ethnic, and religious diversity of a country of more than one billion people; 15 official languages and many dialects; eight major religions; and innumerable sects, castes, classes, and other social divisions. Most Indian languages do not even have a word for a meal. Whereas a person from a Western country might enquire "Have you had lunch (or dinner)," a person from the Subcontinent would ask "Have you eaten bread or (if the person is from a rice-eating area) rice?".

Western meals generally consist of a main course (usually meat or fish), accompanied by smaller side dishes (vegetables, salads), followed by a dessert. An Indian meal is different. There is no 'main course' as such, and meat plays a relatively minor role, even for nonvegetarians. Everything is served at the same time and the dishes remain on the table throughout the meal.

Every Indian meal includes a starch (wheat, rice, millet, sorghum, or corn) and *dal* (boiled spiced lentils). This is supplemented by several dry or wet (curried) vegetable dishes, a little meat or fish, yogurt, and various condiments, including sweet chutneys and sour or hot pickles. In such an arrangement, many dishes compete for attention at the same time and you, the diner, become an active participant in the meal by mixing and matching to create your own flavors. If a dish is too bland, you can add a dab of hot pickle; if it is too spicy, dip your bread in yogurt.

That said, it's better not to mix everything up on your plate but instead eat items one at a time, going back and forth between them if you like and mixing condiments as your taste dictates. The exception is that sauces and gravies can be poured over rice and mixed in with it.

The standard beverage is water. Traditionally, alcohol was not consumed at Indian meals. Drinking beer with Indian meals came from the British and beer has become the drink of choice, especially in the West. However, there is growing interest in drinking wine with Indian food, and we include some suggestions later in this guide.

A Note on Spices

The most distinctive feature of Indian cuisine is the extensive use of spices. Spice is a broad term covering different parts of a plant: fruits or seeds (fennel, mustard, pepper), bark (cinnamon), buds (cloves), stigmas (saffron), roots and rhizomes (turmeric, ginger), even resins (asafetida).

Spices are used in many different ways: they can be ground into a powder called a *masala* (mixture or blend), used whole, or ground with a liquid (yogurt, coconut milk), onions, garlic, or tomatoes to make a paste. Spices are dry roasted or slightly fried to intensify their flavor. They may be added at several points in the cooking process, including the very end.

In Indian food, a home-style vegetable or lentil dish may be made with just a few spices (such as turmeric, cumin and coriander) whereas a sumptuous meat or rice dish prepared by a professional chef may contain twenty or more spices, including aromatic flavorings such as cardamom, cloves, and cinnamon.

In the old days cooks ground spices by hand with a rolling pin and stone slab or in a mortar and pestle. Today ready-made spice powders and pastes sold in

Indian grocery stores make it much easier to prepare Indian dishes at home. Good restaurants prepare their own spice mixtures from scratch.

Typical flavorings include —

North Indian/Pakistani meat and rice: Garlic, green and red chilies, ginger, coriander, black pepper, cumin, green and brown cardamom, cloves, cinnamon, nutmeg, mace, saffron, rose water

Tandoori: Cumin, coriander, cinnamon, cloves, chili powder, ginger, turmeric, garlic

North Indian vegetarian: Coriander, cumin, ginger, onions, garlic, turmeric, green and red chilies, mustard seeds, fenugreek

South Indian: fenugreek, mustard seed, urad dal, cumin, coriander, red chilies, curry leaves

Indian Restaurants in North America

New York (Jackson Heights), Chicago (Devon Avenue), Toronto (Gerard Street), Houston (Hillcroft Avenue), and other North American cities with large South Asian populations have Indian shopping districts with grocery stores, sari and jewelry shops, and restaurants. But you'll also find Indian restaurants in suburban shopping malls, smaller cities and university towns. The majority serve either North Indian/Pakistani dishes or South Indian vegetarian cuisine, but there are some other types of establishments that are worth a visit.

North Indian/Pakistani

Restaurants serving North Indian/Pakistani food are the most common in the United States and Canada. Their standard fare consists of tandoori, meat and rice dishes, and North Indian vegetarian dishes plus a few items from other parts of the Subcontinent, mainly Goa, Bombay, and South India.

Their menus are derived from those in the restaurants that opened after India gained its independence from Britain in 1947. Roadside stands serving street food have always thrived on the Subcontinent, but restaurants with fixed menus and attractive decor that served Indian (not Western) food appeared only in the late 1940s and early 1950s. Their menus featured the hearty vegetarian dishes of North India, such as *sag/palak paneer, mattar paneer* (peas with cheese), *malai kofta* (vegetable balls served in a creamy sauce), *dal makhani* (a rich thick creamy lentil stew), and stuffed *paratha*. (See the glossary pp 31–39 for a definition of these and other terms).

One of the pioneering Indian restaurateurs was Kundan Lal Gujral who created the world's most popular Indian dish: tandoori chicken—pieces of chicken marinated in yogurt and spices and roasted in a tandoor, a free-standing clay oven. In the late 1940s, he opened his restaurant Moti Mahal near the Red Fort in Delhi. It became an overnight sensation and spawned many imitators. Besides tandoori chicken, Moti Mahal's menu featured kabobs—pieces of whole or ground meat, usually lamb, cooked in the tandoor—and all sorts of delicious baked breads. Another Kundan Lal creation was butter chicken (the progenitor of chicken *tikka masala*), pieces of left-over tandoori chicken served in a buttery tomato sauce.

Early restaurants also served dishes associated with North Indian Muslim cuisine, such as *rogan josh* (boneless lamb curry in an aromatic gravy), *korma/ qorma* (braised meat simmered in a yogurt-based sauce), *dopiaza* (meat cooked with a lot of crushed and sliced onions), and *biryani* (an elaborate dish of marinated meat cooked in spices and stock and baked in layers with rice). To make such dishes sound exotic and sophisticated, proprietors called them "Moghlai" after the Moghul emperors who ruled India from the early 16th to the mid 19th centuries. Sometimes the dishes were named after the emperors themselves—Akbari chicken or Shah Jahan biryani. This terminology is a misnomer since these dishes existed long before the Moghuls came to power, although they were raised to new heights of refinement in the emperors' kitchens.

A variation on this style of cooking is the cuisine of the South Indian city of Hyderabad, whose cooks transformed dishes such as *rogan josh* and *korma* by adding coconut milk and local spices such as poppy and caraway seeds.

Hyderabad is famous for its biryanis accompanied by *baigara baingan,* small eggplants cooked in a peanut and sesame seed sauce. A distinctive dessert is *double-ka-keetha,* a very sweet fried bread pudding.

These restaurants generally offer a few dishes from other parts of India, including Bombay street snacks, such as *bhel puri; vindaloo,* a fiery hot and sour meat dish from Goa; Kerala fish dishes (meen mooli); and *idlis, dosas, sambar* and other dishes from South India.

SOUTH INDIAN

Second in popularity are restaurants serving the delicious vegetarian dishes of South India. Small establishments serving strictly vegetarian food have existed in India since the mid-19th century. Many of the cooks got their training in Hindu temples, which served (and still serve) vegetarian dishes to worshippers. The temples in the town of Udupi (also spelled Udipi) were renowned for their food, which is why some South Indian restaurants have the word Udupi in their name.

Idlis

Breakfast is an important meal in South India, and local restaurants opened early in the morning to offer *idlis* (steamed disk-shaped bread made from rice and lentil flour), *dosas* (crepes made from lentil and rice flour), *sambar* (a thin hot and sour dal cooked with vegetables), *vada* (deep fried bread made from lentil and rice flour), *upma* (porridge of semolina or cream of wheat cooked with lentils); and coconut chutney. In the mid-1930s K.K. Rao opened Woodlands restaurant in Madras (today Chennai) to serve South Indian food in a more elegant setting. One of its specialties was an enormous yard-wide paper-thin *dosa.* These breakfast dishes became standard lunch and dinner items in modern South Indian restaurants.

A wonderful nonvegetarian South Indian cuisine is that of the Chettinads, a wealthy trading community famous for its fiery meat and seafood dishes. Chettinad restaurants are located in New Jersey and the suburbs of Toronto.

CHINESE-INDIAN

Restaurants serving an Indianized version of Chinese food are very popular on the Subcontinent and have been transplanted to North America. Typical dishes include chicken corn soup, Manchurian chicken or cauliflower in a garlicky sauce, sweet and sour lamb, and chili chicken. The sauces are colored bright red and heavily flavored with garlic and chili.

DHABAS

These hole-in-the-wall establishments, found mainly in large cities, are popular eating places for taxi drivers from the Subcontinent and Africa. Their menus feature *kabobs, pulaos, biryanis, nihari, paya* (goat trotters), and different kinds of bread. The owners and clientele are largely Muslim; some dhabas have small mosques attached. The menu, featuring delicious, inexpensive food, is sometimes posted on a blackboard.

SWEET AND SNACK SHOPS

Indians love to snack, and an afternoon tea or tiffin featuring salty savories like *samosas* and *pakoras* and countless varieties of sweets are part of daily life. In recent years, shops and cafes serving snacks and sweets have opened in many North American Indian shopping districts.

REGIONAL CUISINES

Large cities also have a few restaurants specializing in food from other parts of India, including the delicious vegetarian cuisine of Gujarat, the seafood creations of Kerala, the hot and sour dishes of Goa, the fiery food of the Chettinads, and the simple, yet delicious, dishes from Nepal. The smaller establishments often close after a few months so if you find one, run, don't walk, to try it out!

Hindu Temples

Usually located in the suburbs of large cities, some Hindu temples (for example, the Hindu Temple of Greater Chicago in Bartlett, Illinois, or the Malibu Hindu Temple near Los Angeles) have their own kitchens where cooks from India prepare South Indian vegetarian dishes on weekends. Visitors are welcome.

Upscale 'Fusion' Restaurants

At secular temples of cuisine such as Vij's in Vancouver, Rasika in Washington, D.C., and Tabla in New York, talented cutting-edge chefs combine Indian and non-Indian techniques and ingredients, with an emphasis on local products. A menu might feature such dishes as Hudson Valley duck curry, braised with caramelized onions and star anise, or Creekstone Farms Beef short rib samosa. These restaurants have extensive wine lists and elegant settings.

Dining Room at Rasika, Washington, DC

Components of a Menu

Soups and Appetizers

Although soups and appetizers are not part of a traditional Indian meal, restaurants include them on their menus. Soups include mulligatawny, a spicy chicken broth; tomato soup; and chicken and corn soup, an Indian-Chinese creation. Although they resemble soups, *dal* and *sambar* are integral parts of a meal and should <u>never</u> be eaten as a first course.

Samosas

The most popular appetizers are *pakoras* or *bhaji* (potatoes, paneer, spinach, cauliflower, or onions deep-fried in a chickpea batter); *samosas* (deep-fried cone-shaped pastries stuffed with potatoes or ground meat); *chaat,* a blend of boiled, diced potatoes and chick peas flavored with lime juice, tamarind, coriander, and spices; *aloo tikki* (potato patties); and *dahi bara* (fried lentil balls in a yogurt sauce.) Sometimes kabobs are served as appetizers.

These dishes may be accompanied by one or more of these sauces for dipping:

- a brown sauce, tamarind-based and slightly sour
- a red sauce, tomato-based and slightly sweet
- a green sauce made from mint, coriander and sometimes chilies.

Spoon a little onto your plate, not on the food, and dip a corner of the appetizer into it as you eat.

Bhelpuri

Some appetizers have their origins in Bombay street food, including *dahi papdi,* crispy wafers topped with yogurt, mint and tamarind sauce and chickpeas; and *bhelpuri* made of crispy noodles, puffed rice, tomato, onion, boiled potatoes, coriander and tamarind chutney.

Pappadums (papads) are fried crispy wafer-like bread made from lentil flour. They, are sometimes placed on the table for diners to nibble on before and during the meal.

Accompaniment: Lassi; beverage of choice.

ENTREES

Vegetable

Gobi

North Indian vegetarian dishes are typically made with cauliflower *(gobi)*, potatoes *(alu/aloo)*, peas *(matar mattar)*, eggplant *(baigun/brinjal)*, okra *(bhindi)*, spinach *(saag/sag or palak)*, chickpeas *(channa)*, and *paneer/panir* (a hard cheese similar to farmer's cheese). They are often cooked in a sauce based on onions and/ or tomatoes. Flavorings include turmeric, cumin seeds, coriander seeds, and fenugreek. Vegetables or *paneer* baked in the tandoor are a good choice for the calorie-conscious.

Accompaniments: A simple bread such as *chapati* or *puri,* plain boiled rice or a vegetable *pulao, dal,* a yogurt and vegetable salad *(raita)*, pickles and chutneys.

In South Indian meals, rice and lentils take center stage. The rice may be plain or flavored with tamarind, lemon, yogurt, tomato, or coconut.

A fermented batter of ground rice and lentils is used to make various South Indian breads, including *idli, dosa,* and *vada,* described in the bread section (p17).

South Indian vegetable dishes include *avial* (vegetables in a creamy coconut sauce); *poriyal,* a dry vegetable dish; *kootu,* a thick stew of vegetables, boiled lentils, and coconut; and *navrattan korma,* mixed vegetables in a coconut gravy.

Poriyal

Accompaniments: South Indian rice and breads are eaten with *sambar,* a *dal* made of lentils, potatoes and other vegetables and/or *rasam,* a thin hot and sour soup-like dal, and coconut chutney. The appropriate drink is sweet milky South Indian coffee if it is available; otherwise, water is fine.

Meat

Meat dishes, often North Indian in origin, are either dry (grilled or roasted) or wet (with a sauce). The spicing is more intense than for vegetable dishes and may include such aromatic spices as cardamom, cinnamon, nutmeg and cloves. Onions and garlic are used in abundance.

Dry dishes include—

- *bihari kabob,* long thin strips of meat marinated in yogurt, papaya, and spices and roasted on skewers

- *boti kabob,* whole chunks of meat marinated in yogurt and/or spices grilled on skewers, also called *tikka kabob*

- *chapli kabob,* a spicy flattened meat patty

- *kofta,* meatballs, sometimes served in a gravy

- *seekh kabob,* ground spiced meat rolled into long cylinders and grilled on skewers

Seekh kabob

- *shammi kabob,* a lightly sautéed patty made of minced meat and ground chickpeas
- tandoori chicken, chicken marinated in yogurt and spices and baked in a clay oven (tandoor).

Accompaniments: These dishes are best eaten with *nans* and *parathas,* an onion and cucumber salad and/or a *raita.* For beverages, see Wines.

Wet meat dishes, sometimes called curries, can be very elaborate. They are often made with lots of onions, garlic, yogurt, cream, nuts, and such aromatic spices as cardamom, cloves, nutmeg and cinnamon. The pieces of meat are simmered slowly in yogurt or another liquid until a thick sauce forms. Dishes in this category include *roghan josh, korma/qorma, dopiaza* ("double onions"), and *achari gosht* (meat with pickles). The meat is generally lamb, goat, or chicken. *Jalfrezi* is a less elaborate dryish meat curry.

Various kabobs at Curry House

Beef may be served in establishments where Hindu prohibitions against eating beef do not apply. A popular and delicious dish (originally eaten at breakfast) is *nihari,* beef shank cooked slowly with ginger, fried onions, green chilies, and aromatic spices until a dark rich gravy is formed. Another is *paya*—goat trotters cooked slowly with spices until a lovely gelatinous gravy results.

Accompaniments: *Paratha* or *nan;* stuffed paratha; *dal, raita.*

Vindaloo

A dish from a different culinary tradition is *vindaloo,* a fiery hot and sour meat dish that originated in Goa, a small state on the West coast of India that was under Portuguese rule for nearly 500 years. (The name comes from the Portuguese *vinho d'alho,* which means wine or wine vinegar and garlic). The original dish was made from pork, a favorite of the Christian Goanese, but restaurants in the West usually make it with lamb, chicken or duck and tone down the hotness and sourness.

Accompaniment: Rice; coconut chutney.

Fish and Seafood

Meen molee

India's coastal states have a rich culinary tradition based on seafood and fish. Kerala in the southwest corner of India is famous for its seafood and fish curries, such as *meen molee,* prepared in a coconut-based sauce. Fish, sautéed in mustard oil and cooked in a gravy, is also a dietary staple in the northeastern state of West Bengal.

Accompaniment: Boiled white rice, chutney.

Tandoori shrimp and fish are more recent additions to restaurant menus.

Accompaniment: *Nan* or *paratha.*

DAL

Dal

The word *dal* means both legumes and the dish made from them. Most Indians, Pakistanis, Bangladeshis and Nepalis eat *dal* every day together with rice, wheat or some other starch.

After the lentils are boiled, they are flavored with a mixture (called a *tarka* or *chauk*) made by frying spices, garlic, onions, chilies or other ingredients in oil or *ghee* and then incorporating this into the cooked dal.

More than fifty kinds of lentils are on the market and they vary in size, shape and color. The most popular are *masur dal,* small salmon-colored disks; yellow *channa dal,* often cooked with meat or vegetables; black *urad dal,* which is ground and soaked to make the batter for South Indian breads; green *moong dal;* and *channa,* or chickpeas (garbanzo beans) that are used whole in curries and salads.

Rice

Most restaurants serve plain white rice *(chawal)*, which goes well with meat or vegetable curries. But more interesting is *pilau* (also spelled *pulao, pullao, pilaf*), a combination of rice and vegetables (often peas) and sometimes meat, chicken or seafood and usually colored yellow. The yellow color may come from saffron (which is very expensive), turmeric, or food coloring.

Pilau

Biryani is a rich, highly aromatic dish of pieces of meat and rice, which, if prepared with care, is the apogee of haute cuisine. A biryani is flavored with many aromatic spices and rose water, and garnished with fried onions, nuts, dried fruits, and even silver foil. There are different ways of making biryani. The rice and meat can be cooked separately, then layered in a sealed pot and cooked slowly in an oven. Alternatively, the meat is first marinated in yogurt and spices, then covered with parboiled rice and cooked over very low heat.

Accompaniment: Biryani is best eaten by itself, perhaps as a separate course following a kabob course. An excellent accompaniment is *bagara baigan,* spicy eggplant in a tomato-based sauce. Otherwise, a simple raita will do.

Bread

Dosas

Breads (rotis) are the glory of the cuisine of the Subcontinent. There are hundreds of varieties, made from different grains and prepared in different ways. The most popular include—

- *appam,* a South Indian bread made from rice flour and coconut milk with a soft interior and crispy edges

- *chapati,* tortilla-like flat breads made from whole wheat flour and cooked over a flame or on an iron pan

- *dosa,* large South Indian crepe-like bread made from fermented rice and lentil batter and lightly sautéed. It may be plain *(sada)* or stuffed with spiced potatoes *(masala dosa),* onions, or other vegetables. *Rava dosa* is made from whole wheat flour

- *idli,* small disc-shaped South Indian bread made of ground fermented rice and lentils and steamed

- *kulcha,* a slightly leavened round wheat bread

- *nan,* a thick round slightly leavened bread made from white flour or a blend of white and whole wheat flour, and baked on the very hot inside of the tandoor

- *paratha,* a multilayered bread made of whole wheat flour and oil and sautéed on a griddle. Parathas may be stuffed with potatoes, onions, and other vegetables

- *peserattu,* a *dosa* made from moong bean flour, often served with *uppuma (upma),* a porridge of semolina or cream of wheat and lentils

- *puri,* small spherical bread made from whole wheat flour and deep fried until it puffs into a sphere.It may be filled with lentils.

Puri

- *sheermal,* a large flakey bread baked in the tandoor and sprinkled with milk and saffron

- *uthappam,* a South Indian pizza-like bread topped with tomatoes and onions

- *vada,* deep-fried south Indian bread that looks like a donut.

Pickles, Chutneys, and Salads

An Indian meal includes several little dishes that complement or contrast with the flavors of the other dishes. Chutneys, usually made of mango and other fruits, are sweet and/or sour and go well with roasted meats. Chutney made from grated coconut is served with South Indian vegetarian dishes.

Mango pickle

Pickles (*achaar*), made from fruit and vegetables, are never sweet and can be sour, salty, hot, or very hot indeed (although rarely in restaurants). The most common ingredients are lime, mango, and mixed vegetables.

Raita is beaten, lightly spiced yogurt containing small pieces of cucumber or other vegetables such as spinach or potatoes. Cool and refreshing, it's a good counterbalance to a fiery dish. A salad of chopped tomatoes and onions lightly flavored with lime and chopped fresh coriander also makes a nice contrast. A western style salad of lettuce is not recommended.

DESSERT

Although Indians have the world's largest collective sweet tooth (sugar refining originated here), a family meal usually ends with fruit or yogurt, not a prepared sweet dish or dessert. Sweet dishes are, however, an integral part of a late-afternoon meal, sometimes called tea, and from here they have found their way into restaurant menus.

Most Indian sweets are made from sugar and milk, which may be either boiled down to form a semi-solid *(khoya)* or thickened or separated by adding a souring agent to make curds *(channa)*. Indian sweet and snack shops offer a large assortment of sweets that you can eat on the spot or take home. The selection in restaurants is much more limited and can include—

- *burfi/barfi,* a hard fudge-like sweet flavored with fruit or nuts

- *firni,* a pudding of ground rice and milk and garnished with nuts

- *gulab jaman,* fried balls of *channa* and sugar in a sweet syrup

Burfi/barfi

- *halwa,* a pudding of grated vegetables (often carrots) cooked with sugar and milk. Indian halwas have a softer texture than Middle Eastern halwas

- *jalebi,* pretzel-like coils of chickpea batter and sugar that are deep fried and then soaked in sugar syrup

Gulab jaman

- *kheer,* a thick rice and milk pudding flavored with cardamom and garnished with nuts and raisins

- *kulfi,* frozen unchurned *khoya* often flavored with mangos or pistachios

- *payasam,* South Indian version of *kheer:* a rice pudding flavored with cardamom and garnished with nuts and sometimes raisins

- *rasmalai,* channa balls cooked in sugar syrup and served in a sweet creamy sauce
- *rasgoola,* channa balls in a sugar syrup
- *sewian,* thin strands of vermicelli fried in ghee, then cooked slowly in milk and flavored with rosewater
- *sheer korma,* a sweet pudding made from vermicelli, milk, saffron, sugar, spices, and ghee
- *shrikand,* a sweet dish made of strained yogurt and flavored with cardamom and saffron. Popular in Western India, it is often sold in grocery stores.

Indians often end a meal by chewing *paan,* a digestive of chopped betel nut, spices, and mineral lime rolled in a betel leaf. *Paan* is sold in some shops, but not usually in restaurants. Most offer their customers *supari,* a mixture of aromatic spices such as fennel, cardamom, and cumin and pieces of candy. *Supari* is believed to sweeten the breath and aid digestion.

BEVERAGES

Lassi

Water is the traditional drink.

Most restaurants serve *lassi,* a yogurt drink, which can be plain (salty) or sweet and flavored with mango. Lassi makes a good starter and can be kept on hand during a meal if you're concerned about hotness since it is so cooling. However, it can be filling. *Nimbu pani,* a delicious drink of lime, water, and salt, is perfect on a hot summer day.

In the Western world, beer has become the drink of choice in Indian restaurants which now often sell beers imported from India. There's nothing really unique about Indian beers, which are brewed in Western-style breweries. Still, if you like beer, an India Pale Ale or a Pilsner hits the spot, especially on a warm day.

The British planted tea in India in the late 19th century and tea drinking became popular in the eastern part of the country, especially Calcutta, where afternoon tea is a ritual and tea is drunk with milk and sugar—never spices! Chai, which is tea boiled with milk and spices, was actively promoted by the Indian Tea Board in the 1950s as a way of using a surplus of inferior tea.

In South India, coffee is the drink of choice. It is a strong sweet milky beverage resembling cafe au lait brewed in a filter device.

Wine and Indian Food

Pairing wines with Indian food is challenging and controversial. Since an Indian meal is such a mélange of flavors and spices, and because people to some degree mix and match the components to suit their own tastes, it's difficult finding a wine that goes with every part of the meal.

Samosas paired with wine

Some wine experts recommend *gewürztraminer* ("spicy grape" in German) on the theory that its aromatic nature enhances the spices in Indian cuisine, especially ginger and cardamom, while its sweetness tones down the spiciness. Sometimes this works, but sometimes it does not and the wine clashes with the flavors of the food.

Dry white wines such as pinot blanc and pinot gris can be a good match for vegetable and seafood dishes, especially those with a yogurt- or cream-based gravy. For meat, it's best to avoid oaky heavy reds like cabernet sauvignon which clash with the spicing, and keep to lighter wines with lower alcohol content (14% or less.)

A fruity pinot noir, zinfandel, or shiraz are good matches for tandoori dishes such as kabobs, tandoori chicken, and grilled paneer. Fruity wines go especially well with lamb. Rosés, especially those made from Cabernet Franc, are versatile and go well with many dishes, including shammi kabobs.

The Health Benefits of Indian Food

Modern science is confirming what Indian doctors have known for thousands of years: the health benefits of spices. Cinnamon has been shown to lower LDL cholesterol and blood sugar for people with Type 2 diabetes, relieve arthritis pain, and boost memory.

Ginger improves digestion, lowers cholesterol levels, and helps to stabilize blood pressure and blood glucose levels.

Chilies are especially beneficial because of their antibacterial and anti-inflammatory properties—and they may also speed up your metabolism. Chilies are also rich in Vitamin C.

However, the king of the health-enhancing spices is turmeric, a key component in Indian vegetarian dishes and the ingredient that gives curry powder its yellow color. Studies show that people whose diet regularly includes turmeric have lower rates of breast, prostate, lung and colon cancers and childhood leukemia than people who are not turmeric-eaters.

Alzheimer's disease is rarer in India and Singapore than in the West, especially among older adults who have eaten turmeric-rich dishes for most of their lives. Regular consumption of turmeric may prevent, slow down or even cure chronic maladies, ranging from indigestion and cold sores to diabetes, cancer, multiple sclerosis, arthritis, and heart disease.

For Those Watching Their Calories ...

Indians generally use a lot of oil or clarified butter (*ghee*) in their cooking, even in vegetable dishes, so it's safer to stick to dry roasted dishes like meat or vegetable kabobs and tandoori chicken, accompanied by chapatis. Usually salads are oil free.

General Guidelines for Ordering

1. If available, order a thali (a combination of dishes) on a first visit.

2. Share dishes with others at the table.

3. Stay within a regional tradition (e.g., South or North).

4. Balance wet and dry dishes.

5. Balance hot (i.e., containing pepper or chilies) and cooling (i.e., yogurt) dishes.

6. Balance different meats, seafood and vegetables when selecting courses

7. Order simple breads and rice dishes with vegetable dishes and richer breads with meat dishes.

Above all, enjoy your meal!

Some Sample Meals
(to be shared at table)

For additional diners, add one more dish per two people, keeping in mind the principles on the previous page.

NORTH INDIAN

Two people (non-vegetarian)

Samosas
or
Shammi kabob

Tandoori chicken (dry)
or
Lamb seekh kabob
Nan

Chicken tikka masala (wet)
or
Lamb korma
Paratha

Raita

Dal

Rice (optional)

Mango or pistachio kulfi
or
Gulab jaman

Two people (vegetarian)

Vegetable Samosas
or
Pakoras
or
Bhelpuri

Tandoori paneer (dry)
or
Tandoori vegetables
Nan

Malai kofta (wet)
or
Vegetable korma/navrattan
or
Mattar paneer

Vegetable pulao (optional)

Dal

Raita

Carrot halwa
or
Rasmalai

Four People (Non-vegetarian)   Four People (Vegetarian)

Meat Samosas
or
Shammi kabob
Lassi

Boti kabob (dry)
or
Seekh kabob
Nan

Chicken curry (wet)
or
Chicken tikka masala
Paratha

Tandoori shrimp + nan
or
Fish or shrimp molee + rice

Dal

Raita

Mango or pistachio kulfi
Rasmalai

For additional diners, add chicken or
lamb biryani with bagara baigan

Vegetable samosa
Bhelpuri
Lassi

Tandoori vegetables (dry)
or Paneer kabob
Nan

Malai kofta (wet)

Saag paneer

Vegetable pulao

Dal

Raita

Carrot halwa
Gulab jaman

South Indian (Vegetarian)

Two people	Four people
Idlis or dosa (plain or masala)	Rasam
Sambar	Idlis
Coconut chutney	Masala dosa
Papads	Sambar
Payasam	Coconut chutney
South Indian coffee (if available)	Papaddums
	Two vegetable curries (avial, navrat-tan) with plain boiled rice
	Payasam
	South Indian coffee (if available)

FAQ

Will Indian food burn my mouth? And what should I do if it does?

The intensive use of spices is the defining characteristic of Indian cuisine. However, it's important to distinguish between 'spicy' and 'hot.' 'Hotness'—a burning sensation in the mouth—comes from black peppers, which are native to India, and from chilies, which were introduced by the Portuguese in the 16th century. 'Spiciness', characterized by aroma and complexity, comes from so-called 'brown' spices such as cumin, coriander, fenugreek, and mustard seeds, which are used to flavor many vegetable dishes, and aromatic spices — cloves, cinnamon, mace, and cardamom seeds — used in many meat preparations.

In North America, most mainstream Indian restaurants err on the side of mildness, so if you enjoy 'hot' food, ask the waiter to spice up your dish. (Hint: Often the word "Madras" in the name of a dish means it is on the hot side.) If you accidentally bite into a chili and feel your mouth is on fire, eat a piece of bread or some rice or drink milk or yogurt which will relieve the pain more effectively than water or beer.

What's a curry?

The British borrowed the word 'curry' from the Tamil *kari* meaning a thin sauce poured over rice and used it as a catchall for any Indian dish of meat, fish or vegetables with a gravy. Traditionally, the word was not used by Indians, who called dishes by their specific names. However, in recent years it has become more acceptable, and many Indians now use the word for any stew-like dish, a practice we follow in this guide.

Curry powder is a ready-made blend of spices invented by the British in the 19th century to make it easier to prepare Indian dishes. It is rarely used in restaurants. The main ingredients in a curry powder are turmeric, cumin, coriander, chilies, and fenugreek. Some purists frown upon the use of curry powder for home cooking but it is useful if you want to prepare a curry in a hurry. The kind sold in Chinese grocery stores is close to the original British version.

Is Indian food only for vegetarians?

Contrary to what many people believe, the majority of Indians are not vegetarians, and very few Indians are vegans: Milk and milk products are important dietary components. Still, meat is eaten sparingly by most people, even non-vegetarians, and is one among many components of a meal rather than the centerpiece, as it is in the West.

Eating beef is taboo among Hindus, while Muslims avoid pork, so these two meats are rarely served. The most commonly offered meats are lamb and chicken and occasionally goat. Some people are squeamish about eating goat meat, but it is delicious and not at all 'barnyardy.'

Should I try the buffet?

By all means! Many Indian dishes are cooked for long periods of time and their taste and texture don't suffer by being kept warm on a steam table. The typical buffet includes a good selection of dishes for vegetarians and nonvegetarians: tandoori chicken (sometimes

Buffet at Indian Harvest Restaurant

prepared fresh and delivered to your table), one or two dals, vegetable pulao, several vegetable dishes, one or two meat curries, and one or two desserts.

What's the correct way to eat Indian food?

A traditional Indian meal is served on a *thali*—a circular metal tray with small bowls. Bread and/or rice are placed on the tray along with the condiments, while curries and dals are served in the bowls. Thali is also the name of a meal served in this way. Most restaurants offer vegetarian or non-vegetarian thalis, which contain all the main components of a meal.

Using a spoon and fork to eat an Indian meal is perfectly acceptable. Traditionally, Indians ate without utensils using only their right hands. (The left hand is considered unclean and not used at the table). This is fairly easy when the accompaniment is bread. You break off a small piece, wrap it around a piece of meat or vegetable, dip it in the gravy and any condiments that strike your fancy, and pop it into your mouth. It takes a bit of practice but is easy to master. Like using chopsticks to eat Chinese food, this somehow makes the food taste better!

Eating rice with your hands is a lot trickier. You take a small piece of rice using the tips of your fingers, mix it with some food, and pop it into your mouth. Etiquette requires that the liquid not run up your wrist or arm, which isn't easy to avoid if you're not used to it.

Glossary Of Some Common Terms

This glossary provides brief descriptions of the ingredients and dishes most often found on Indian restaurant menus.

One of the problems in writing about Indian food is that many dishes do not have precise names. For example, a vegetable dish may be described as *bhaji*, which simply means sautéed vegetables. Moreover, there may be considerable variation in the way that a dish is prepared and the ingredients that go into it, especially the spices.

The names of dishes are transcribed from Hindi and other Indian languages, which are written in non-Roman scripts. Because menu-writers adopt their own methods of transcription (and because many sounds have no exact English equivalent) there are wide—and sometimes very imaginative!—variations in the names of dishes. I've used the most common spellings and have given some alternatives in parentheses.

Aam/am: Mango

Achar/achaar: Vegetable or fruit pickles ranging from mild to very hot and often sour

Adrak: Ginger

Aloo/alu: Potato

Anda: Eggs

Appam: Crepes made from rice flour and coconut milk with a soft interior and a crispy rim. (Sometimes called hoppers. South Indian, especially Kerala)

Avial: Mixed vegetables in a coconut milk gravy (South Indian)

Badam/badaam: Almonds or stuffed with almonds

Bagara baigan: Small eggplants cooked in a peanut and sesame seed sauce. An accompaniment to biryani

Baigan/baingan: Eggplant

Baingan bharta: Roasted and pureed eggplant

Balti: Stir-fried vegetables: meat or seafood in a sauce of onions, ginger, tomatoes, and spices prepared and served in a wok-line pan called a karhai. Invented in the U.K.

Burfi/barfi: Fudge-like sweet

Bhaji: Deep-fried vegetables in a batter (see pakora)

Bhelpuri: Snack made of puffed rice, tomato, onion, boiled potatoes, coriander and tamarind

Bhindi: Okra

Bhoona (bhuna) gosht: A dry meat curry

Bihari kabob: Long thin strips of meat marinated in yogurt and roasted on skewers

Biryani: Elaborate dish of marinated meat cooked in spices and stock, baked in layers with rice

Bisi bhele bhat: Rice, lentils, and vegetables. (South Indian, especially Karnataka)

Boti kabob: Chunks of meat marinated in yogurt and grilled on skewers. Also called tikka kabob

Brinjal: Eggplant

Butter chicken: Pieces of tandoori chicken in a rich tomato sauce

Cha/chai: Tea; often used for spiced tea (also called *masala chai*)

Chaat/chat: Generic term for salty snacks

Chapli kabob: Flattened spicy meat patty

Channa dal: Yellow split peas

Channa: Chick peas (garbanzos)

Chapati: Flat round unleavened whole wheat bread cooked on a hot griddle with no or little oil

Chawal: Plain boiled white rice

Chettinad: Wealthy South Indian trading community famous for their fiery meat and seafood dishes

Chicken tikka masala: Pieces of chicken baked in a tandoor and served in a creamy tomato sauce

Chili chicken: Batter-fried chicken sautéed with onion and green chilies, sometimes served in a soy and ginger sauce. A popular Indian-Chinese dish

Chingri: Shrimp or prawns

Chutney (chatni): Sweet, sometimes slightly sour, condiment or relish made from a variety of ingredients such as mangoes, tomatoes, mint, coconut, etc.

Curry leaves/kari patta: Leaves from a shrub used as a flavoring, especially vegetable dishes and dals

Dahi: Yogurt (called curd in India)

Dahi bara: Fried lentil balls in a yogurt sauce

Dahi papdi: Crispy wafers topped with yogurt, mint and tamarind sauce and chickpeas

Dal/dhal: Collective term for dried peas and lentils and the boiled dish made from them

Dal makhani: Lentils simmered in a tomato and cream sauce

Dhania: Coriander

Dhansak: Chicken or lamb cooked with lentils, spices, and various vegetables such as spinach and eggplants. (A Parsi dish)

Dhokla: Steamed cake made of dal flour. (A popular Gujarati snack)

Dopiaza/dopiyaza (literally, 'double onions'): Beef or lamb cooked with a lot of crushed and sliced onions

Dosa: Large crepe-like bread made from a batter of ground lentils rice flour. (South Indian)

Dum: Steamed

Dumpukht/dumpokht: A steamed dish, usually made of meat. (Associated with the city Lucknow)

Firni: Sweet milk pudding thickened with rice flour or cornflour and flavored with rosewater and aromatic spices such as cardamom

Gajjar: Carrots

Garam masala: Spice mixture

Ghee/ghi: Clarified butter

Gobi: Cauliflower

Gosht: Meat

Gulab jamun: Fried balls of thickened milk and sugar in a sweet syrup

Haldi: Turmeric. Bright yellow spice used in many vegetable and lentil dishes

Halwa: Pudding usually made from sugar and grated vegetables, especially carrots

Haleem/halim: Slowly cooked porridge-like dish of cracked wheat and other grains, meat and spices

Hare: Green (color)

Hing: Asafoetida; ground resin used as a substitute for garlic in dals and vegetable dishes

Idli: Steamed disk-shaped bread made from rice and lentil flour. (South Indian)

Imli: Tamarind; a sour flavoring

Jaiphal: Nutmeg

Jalebi: Pretzel-like coils of chickpea batter and sugar deep fried and soaked in sugar syrup

Jalfrezi: Stir-fried dry meat or vegetable dish

Jaljeera: Cumin-flavoured cold drink

Jeera (zeera): Cumin seed

Jhinga, jhingri: Shrimp, prawns

Kabob/kabab: Minced or cubed meat cooked over a grill or in a tandoor

Kachori/kachauri: Small deep-fried pastries filled with lentils

Kachumber: Vegetable salad

Kadhi/karhi: Chickpea and buttermilk curry

Kaju: Cashew

Kali mirch: Black pepper

Karela: Bitter gourd

Keema/qima: Minced meat (lamb or beef)

Keema mattar: Minced meat and peas

Kheer: Thick sweet rice and milk pudding

Khichri/Khichdi: Cooked rice and dal garnished with fried onions

Khumb: Mushrooms

Kofta: Ground meat or paneer formed into small balls and roasted in a tandoor or prepared in a gravy

Kootoo: Thick stew of vegetables, boiled lentils and coconut. (South Indian)

Korma/qorma: A dish of braised meat simmered in a mild but aromatic yogurt-based sauce.

Kulcha: Slightly leavened round bread

Kulfi: Frozen unchurned thickened and sweetened milk: often flavored with mangos and pistachios

Lal: Red

Madras or Madras curry: A dish made with coconut milk, chilies and curry leaves. Madras curries have a reputation for being 'hot'.

Mach/maach/maachi/machli: Fish

Makhan: Butter

Makhani: Dish made with butter, cream and tomatoes

Maki ki roti: Corn bread

Malai: Cream

Malai kabobs: Chicken marinated in cream and spices

Malai kofta: Vegetable balls served in a creamy sauce

Manchurian chicken: Pieces of chicken in a garlic sauce. (Indian-Chinese)

Masaledar: Stir-fried

Masala: Spices; a spicy gravy

Masoor dal: Red lentils

Mattar: Peas

Meen: Fish (South Indian)

Methi: Fenugreek

Milikai podi: A dry blend of spices and chilies served with South Indian dishes

Mirch: Peppers or chilies

Moghul/Moghlai: A specious term applied to some North Indian/Pakistani dishes, intended to give the impression of great luxury and sophistication

Molee/moolee: Fish or seafood cooked in coconut. (South Indian)

Momos: Steamed dumplings filled with meat or vegetables. (Nepali/Tibetan)

Mooli/moolee: White radish

Moong dal: Green lentils

Mulligatawny soup: Chicken soup flavored with spices and tamarind paste created by the British.

Murgh makhani: Roasted chicken in a rich tomato and butter sauce

Murgh/moorg/murghi: Chicken

Murgh massalam: Whole chicken marinated in yogurt and filled with rice, peas, and egg

Naan/nan: Thick tear-shaped slightly leavened bread baked on the side of the tandoor

Nariyal: Coconut

Navrattan: Literally, "nine jewels," mixed vegetables

Nihari: Pieces of beef slow-cooked with ginger and spices

Nimbu: Lemon or lime

Nimbu pani: Refreshing drink of lime, water, and salt

Pakoras: Onions, potatoes, cauliflower, and other vegetables deep-fried in a chickpea batter

Palak: Spinach

Palak gosht: Dryish curry of lamb and spinach

Paneer/panir: Hard farmer's cheese, used as an ingredient in North Indian vegetarian dishes

Pappadums/papads: Crispy fried or baked wafers made from lentils and rice flour batter

Paratha/parantha: Multilayered bread made of whole wheat flour and oil and sautéed on a griddle

Pasanda: Thin slices of meat, usually lamb

 Pasanda gosht: thin slices of lamb in a mild sauce

Peserattu: Dosa made from moong bean flour

Peshwari nan: Nan stuffed with dried fruit

Phool gobi: Cauliflower

Pista: Pistachio

Podina/pudina: Mint

Puri/poori: Puffy round deep-fried wheat bread

Pullao/pilaos/pilav: Rice sautéed in onions and spices, then boiled with water or stock, and mixed with chicken, meat, or vegetables. Usually colored yellow.

Pyaz/piaz: Onions

Raan/ran: Whole leg of lamb

Raita: Yogurt salad with small pieces of cucumber, cooked potato, or other vegetables. A standard 'cooling' accompaniment.

Rajma: Kidney beans

Rasam: Thin highly seasoned lentil broth. (South Indian)

Ras malai: Disks of cheese cooked in sugar syrup and served with a sweet creamy sauce

Ravi: Semolina or cream of wheat

Roghan/rogan josh: Boneless lamb curry in an aromatic gravy

Roti: General term for bread. Sometimes used interchangeably with chapati.

Saag: Spinach or mustard greens

Saagwala: Meat or seafood in a spinach sauce.

Sabzi: Vegetables

Sada: Plain (as in sada chawal, boiled white rice)

Safid: White

Sambar: Thin hot and sour South Indian dal cooked with vegetables

Samosa: Baked or fried triangular pastries filled with spiced minced meat or potatoes

Sarson: Mustard greens

Seekh kabob: Ground spiced meat rolled into long cylinders and grilled on skewers

Sevian: Vermicelli noodles

Shami kabob: Patties made of meat and ground lentils

Shalgam: Turnip

Shammi kabob: Lightly sautéed small meat patty made of minced meat and ground split peas

Sheermal/shirmal: Large flakey reactangular wheat bread baked in the tandoor and sprinkled with milk and saffron

Shorba: Soup

Shrikand: Sweet dish made of strained yogurt and flavored with cardamom and saffron. (West Indian)

Sooji/soji: Semolina

Suka/sookha: Dish that is dry and lightly spiced

Supari: Mixture of aromatic spices such as fennel, cardamom and cumin mixed with pieces of candy. An after dinner digestive/breath freshener

Tandoor: Clay oven

Tandoori: A dish baked in a tandoor

Thali: Round metal plate with little bowls on which Indian meals are served. Also the name of the meal

Tikka: Pieces of meat or fish marinated in yogurt and spices and baked in a tandoor

Til: Sesame seed or sesame oil

Toor/toovar dal: Yellow lentils

Uppuma/upma: Porridge of semolina or cream of wheat cooked with lentils. (South Indian)

Urad dal: Black lentils

Vada: Donut-like bread made of rice and lentils and deep fried. (South Indian)

Vindaloo: Sour and 'hot' meat curry. In theory it is very hot but usually tamed down in North American restaurants. (Goan)

Answers to back cover questions:

1. Eat some bread or rice or drink milk

2. Tandoori chicken

3. Dal (boiled lentils)

4. A fruity red wine, such as zinfandel or pinot noir

5. Rice and coconut chutney

6. Anything from the tandoor

7. A key ingredient in curry powder and curries is turmeric, which has anti-inflammatory properties.

Made in the USA
Charleston, SC
04 August 2010